NATIONAL
GEOGRAPH

# Light

Monica Halpern

# Contents

# Light for Life

Look around you. What do you see? Friends smiling?
Sunshine? Beautiful colors? The words on this page?
Now imagine a world without light. What could you see?
Nothing! You need light to see.

Besides making the world a beautiful place, light is
necessary for every living thing. Without light, plants don't
grow. And without plants, animals and people would have
no food.

# Sources of Light

Light is a form of energy that lets us see people and objects. Most objects do not give off light on their own. You see them only when light from another source bounces off them and into your eyes.

## Natural Light

Anything that gives off light is a **light source**. Light comes from many different sources. Some sources of light are natural, such as the sun and other stars.

Most light on Earth comes from the sun, our nearest star. The sun is our most important source of light and heat. Without sunlight, Earth would be a cold, dark place. Nothing could live here.

**Be Careful!**

Never look straight at the sun, even if you are wearing sunglasses. You could hurt your eyes very badly or even go blind!

The sun is a huge ball of very hot gases. The sun gives off huge amounts of heat and light.

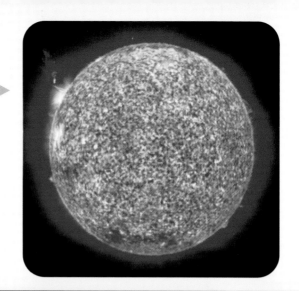

# Artificial Sources of Light

When it is dark outside, we use artificial sources of light. Candles, flashlights, and lamps are artificial sources of light. Long ago, people probably used campfires for light. Later, people used candles, oil lamps, and gas lamps. Today, electricity is our main source of artificial light.

People once used oil lamps for light.

**Did You Know?**

Thomas Edison made the first electric light in 1879. That invention let people do more things at night.

# Animals and Light

Some animals produce their own light. Have you ever seen a firefly at night? Fireflies give off a yellow light. Certain fish deep in the ocean also produce light. The lantern fish and the hatchetfish produce light to communicate.

▼ A glowworm gives off a green light.

# Moving Light

Try this experiment to see how light travels in a straight line.

## Here's What You Need

* a flashlight
* 2-3 pieces of newspaper
* baking soda
* a friend

## Here's What You Do

1. Spread the newspaper on the floor.
2. Make the room dark.
3. Turn the flashlight on.
4. Shine it across the newspaper.
5. Ask a friend to sprinkle baking soda over the beam of light. Do you see the beam of light?

The beam of light ▶

# The Speed of Light

Light travels very fast. You can't see light moving. Light rays travel at about 186,000 miles per second (300,000 kilometers per second). It takes only about eight minutes for light from the sun to reach you.

Light travels much faster than sound. That's why during a storm you will see a flash of lightning several seconds before you hear a clap of thunder.

▼ Lightning is a huge spark of electricity that gives off light.

# Bouncing and Bending Light

Sources, such as the sun or a light bulb, give off their own light. We can see other objects when light bounces off them.

## Reflected Light

You can see an object because light hits the object and **reflects**, or bounces back, to your eyes. A mirror reflects light very well. That's because it is smooth and shiny. When light hits something that is rough and dark, such as a piece of wood, much less light bounces back.

▼ This smooth, shiny lake reflects light bouncing off the mountains and trees.

# Passing Through

Some materials let light pass through them. Think of light streaming through the windows in your classroom. Materials that let nearly all light pass through them are **transparent**. You can see through them. Clean air, clean water, and clear glass are transparent.

Materials that let only some light pass through them are **translucent**. They make things look cloudy or fuzzy. Wax paper is translucent.

▼ The windows in vehicles are transparent so drivers can see where they are going. This is a train driver's view.

# Refracting Light

When light passes through an object, it slows down a little. It also bends, or changes direction. When light bends, we say it **refracts**.

Light travels faster through air than it does through water or glass. Think about how water slows you down when you try to walk through it. Water slows light down, too. When light enters the water, the light rays slow down and refract, or bend. A pencil in a glass of water appears to be broken because of refraction.

It looks like the pencil is broken because the light bouncing off the pencil refracts, or bends, as it enters the water.

# A Magic Coin

Try this experiment to see how refraction works.

## Here's What You Need

* a coin
* water
* a large bowl
* tape
* a friend

## Here's What You Do

1. Tape the coin to the bottom of the bowl.
2. Put the bowl on a table.
3. Keep looking at the coin as you slowly back away from the table.
4. Stop when you can't see the coin.
5. Ask a friend to pour water into the bowl. What happens?

You will find that you can see the coin again! The light from the coin is refracted, or bent, by the water so much that you can see it again.

# Making Shadows

Light can pass through some materials, such as glass and clear plastic. But light cannot pass through all materials. Materials that do not let light pass through are **opaque**.

What happens when light hits an opaque object? The object blocks the light. Light travels in straight lines. It cannot bend around objects in its path. When an object blocks the light, a shadow is formed. A shadow is an area of darkness that forms when light is blocked by an object.

The apple is blocking the light. This makes a shadow.

# You and Your Shadow

On a sunny day, you can see your own shadow. Wherever you go, you will have a shadow because light cannot pass through your body. When the sun is behind you, your shadow will be in front of you. When the sun is in front of you, where do you think your shadow will be?

Do shadows stay the same all day? No, shadows change as the position of the source of light changes. Early in the day, shadows will be long. This is because the sun is low in the sky. In the middle of the day, the sun is high in the sky. It will make short shadows. Late in the day, the sun is low in the sky again. What kind of shadows do you think it will make?

## Did You Know?

A sundial uses the shadow cast by the sun to show the time. The first sundials were used by the Chinese more than 4,000 years ago. There is one problem with sundials. They don't work on a cloudy day.

▲ Shadows are long early in the day.

▲ Shadows are short in the middle of the day.

# Light and Color

Have you ever seen a rainbow in the sky? You might have seen one just after a rain shower. The colors in a rainbow—red, orange, yellow, green, blue, indigo, and violet—seem to blend together. They form a **spectrum**, or range, of colors. In a rainbow, the same colors always appear in the same order.

## Wavelengths

Scientists have learned that light travels in waves. Waves have wavelengths. A **wavelength** is the distance from the top of one wave to the top of the next.

Each color of the spectrum has its own wavelength. Violet has the shortest wavelength. Red has the longest. All the other colors are somewhere in between. Our eyes see these different wavelengths as different colors.

When you look around you, you see many colors. You see green trees, red apples, yellow buses, and blue mailboxes. Light allows us to see many different colors.

How do we see colors? A blue mailbox has paint that reflects only the wavelengths that you see as blue. The paint **absorbs**, or soaks up, all the other colors. The wavelengths of blue are not absorbed. Instead, they are reflected to your eyes. That's why you see a blue mailbox.

▲ The colors you see depend on the way light is absorbed and reflected.

# Making a Rainbow

Try this experiment to see if you can make a rainbow.

## Here's What You Need

* a bucket
* water
* liquid detergent
* 2-3 tablespoons of sugar
* thin wire that bends, such as a wire coat hanger

## Here's What You Do

1. Make up a soap solution in the bucket with the water and detergent.
2. Add the sugar to thicken the solution.
3. Bend the wire into a simple rounded shape, leaving a piece of wire as a handle.
4. Dip the shaped wire into the soap solution.
5. Pull it out slowly. Do you see a rainbow?

Now you know how important light is to your world. Without it, the world would be a cold, dark, and dreary place. There would be no sunshine. There would be no colors. There would be no rainbows.

So keep looking around you. Think about how the bouncing and bending of light helps to make your world a more beautiful place. And enjoy what you see!

# Glossary

**absorb**        to take in or soak up

**light source**        something that gives off light

**opaque**        letting no light pass through

**reflect**        to bounce off a surface, such as light off a mirror

**refract**        to bend when passing through a substance, such as light through water

**spectrum**        a range of colors, including red, orange, yellow, green, blue, indigo, and violet

**translucent**        letting some light pass through

**transparent**        letting most light pass through

**wavelength**        the distance from the top of one wave to the top of the next wave

# Index